Seppuku Quarterly

Seppuku Quarterly

Seppuku Quarterly/Joseph Fulkerson
ISBN: 979-8-9855916-5-1
Laughing Ronin Press

sep·pu·ku /ˈsepo͞oˌko͞o, səˈpo͞oˌko͞o/

(Japanese: 切腹, "cutting [the] belly"), sometimes referred to as harakiri is a form of Japanese ritual suicide by disembowelment.

It was favoured under Bushidō (warrior code) as an effective way to demonstrate the courage, self-control, and strong resolve of the samurai and to prove sincerity of purpose.

A special thanks to all the contributors to this journal, and to those of future iterations.

Demon
Clyde Liffey

Once full, now nearly empty, I cradled the tumbler in my hand, gazed out the window, wondered how I'd return, this building has corridors surpassing mental maps. One of the women in the courtyard wore a tight patterned sundress that clung to her buttocks as she rose from the lawn chair. I leaned over to get a better look, felt something pressing against my groin.

"Demon, stop!" the owner said.

I turned. I'd seen her, always in a long billowing dress, and her dog at various parks in the city. "I'm so sorry," she said, extending a hand. "Demon's always too friendly with people he likes."

Uneasy, I stammered something to put her at her ease. She didn't need my help. White-haired, wrinkled, thin, there was a *nous ne savons pas* about her that was more alluring than the voluptuous women lounging in the courtyard.

"How do you know V?" she asked.

I still don't know V. I'd come to the opening just because, wandered here after slipping through a door that was left ajar. I figured I'd have a glass of wine or two, dawdle a while, maybe learn something about painting, go back to my apartment. I shouldn't have poured myself that second glass, shouldn't have filled it to the brim, should have eaten lunch.

Ever tactful, she led me back to the gallery. She paused before opening the door. "I wonder if you could do a favor for me. I just met a dear sweet man," she explained. "He's from Switzerland, a diplomat or banker, maybe both. He asked me to accompany him. He seems so forlorn. I can't take Demon with me. Here's my keys and," she wrote on her stationery, "my address. If you'd just take Demon home and make sure his water bowl is filled." She placed a bill into my shirt pocket.

I took the leash, she returned to her diplomat. Still unsteady from drinking on an empty stomach, I grabbed a handful of nuts and circuited the paintings. I stopped before a sketch of some spaniels. There was a mark near it indicating that it was sold.

A tall young couple were admiring it. "I hear your friend the widow just bought it," the woman said to me.

I tried to be blasé. "Really, who drew it?"

"Courbet," the man said, suppressing a snicker.

"Come, Demon, let's get some fresh air."

I picked the bill out of my pocket as I cleaned up next morning. It was a fifty.

An hour or two later I sat on my usual bench in Riverside Park. "Let's go to brunch," I said, "my treat."

April took a yogurt out of her handbag. "Save your money," she said, "at least till you get a replacement apartment-mate."

"But I need a drink."

"Hair of the dog?"

"Yes."

She fed me a spoonful of yogurt. "Try this. If you still need a drink, I think I have some gin in a cabinet somewhere."

I waved the fifty, told her how I'd acquired it.

"So you finally spoke to your mysterious widow?" April said, unimpressed.

"I've petted her dog before." She was silent. Just then we saw a man with a decathlete's build finish his jog. He stretched against a low fence with iron railings. A little white dog nipped at his socks. The young woman holding the leash apologized. He grinned his Wheaties box grin, took hold of the leash, they walked off together.

"That's meeting cute," April commented. "Your meeting sounds ghastly."

"It was just a chance encounter."

The next week, April asked me about the widow's date.

"She told me it was fine," I said. "He's gone now, back to Switzerland I suppose."

That meeting with the widow led to a business relation. The weather was getting warmer, many of her friends were spending weekends in the Hamptons or Newport.

Sometimes their dogs stayed behind. Just because I walked Demon home, refilled his water bowl, and didn't steal anything from her apartment, the widow referred me to them. I didn't mind. New York was more expensive than I anticipated, in the fall I planned to start business school, I needed the money.

About a month after my business started, I sat with April on our bench. She had a copy of Friday's *Times*. She showed me a headshot in the business section.

"That's the man who dated the widow," I said.

"I know," April said. "'Victor Lavaliere, the esteemed Swiss diplomat and banker, was found dead. He was last seen at a private opening at the posh V gallery on Madison Avenue. The autopsy found no evidence of foul play. He died of unknown natural causes.' Doesn't that make you suspicious?"

I don't know why April didn't like the widow, just female jealousy, I guess. My relations or lack thereof with the old woman strained our relation. "It's just a strange coincidence," I finally replied. "Anyway, I'm quitting before

Labor Day weekend. I'll take you to that fancy Cuban restaurant to celebrate."

The summer passed. April spent two weeks with her family in Ohio and Kentucky, I stayed in New York, taking an occasional day off if my side gig called for it. My clients wished me well, hoped I'd resume services next May.

My company let us off early the Friday of Labor Day weekend. I stopped at a deli in the Village to pick up some supplies for a picnic April and I planned with some friends. I'd just placed my order when I turned to see the widow. It was the first time I saw her without her dog.

"I have a favor to ask you," she said.

"I'm sorry, I"

"It's not dog-sitting. Demon can care for himself. I had a date for the gala on the tenth but, well, Purdy Baldwin is standing me up."

"Isn't he?"

"He's"

"Of course, but," before I could say anything further, she hugged me. I felt her bony skin against my side, her soft still firm breasts against my ribs. Despite our age difference I was aroused. She noted my excitement, patted my tush, and said, "It's a date. Pick me up at seven.
It's black tie of course. Whatever you do, don't tell your little girlfriend about it."

The deli clerk yelled for me to take my things off the counter. I swept them into my basket, turned toward the cashier. The widow was gone.

I rented a tuxedo on short notice, still had enough left over to treat April to a fancy Cuban dinner.

It was our first time at the restaurant. I expected her to be excited. She was subdued. "Another season is starting," she said.

"Yes, I thought I'd learn a lot about the arts when I moved to New York but now that things are starting up again, I'll be spending most of my time working and studying."

"You're not missing much."

"You can say that. You work in the art world." I observed the widow's dictum about the gala. April wouldn't be working it: I was sure the widow made sure of that.

"At least you'll be away from the widow's shadowy world."

"What do you mean?"

"I suppose I should have told you earlier, but you seemed to enjoy your dog-walking business so much."

"I grew up with dogs. It's a connection."

"You didn't notice anything unusual about the widow's love life?"

"She never seemed to date anyone more than once or twice. I guess she was unlucky or just picky."

"It seems that everyone she's been with in the four or five months she's lived here has either died or disappeared. Victor Lavaliere is just the most prominent. She transmitted something to all of them, even those who used protection. She uses that dog to sniff out and attract her victims."

"How do you know this?"

"I was a zoology major before I switched."

"With a minor in parapsychology."

"If that's how you feel"

"Just joking."

"I abandoned zoology because science can only go so far. We have our senses but they can't detect every aspect of the world. Dogs"

We'd had this conversation before. April's mention of dogs set me thinking once again of the difference between the hounds and mutts April and I grew up with and the pedigrees and special crosses owned by the widow's set. I sipped my wine. A remnant of the widow's radiance still enveloped me, prevented me from fully engaging with April.

"Of course if you're not going to listen," April finished.

"I'm sorry. It's been a long week. I'm worried about my course load."

"It's better for you to study with people your own age than be a lackey to those strange jet set dowagers you hooked up with."

"I suppose." April picked at her food, I devoured mine but didn't enjoy it. I walked her home, kissed her perfunctorily, she responded passionately, we spent the night at her place.

I rose early the next morning so I could shower and pick up the picnic supplies at my apartment. April squeezed my wrist before I left. "We may not get a private moment at the picnic. Promise me you won't see any of those women, especially the widow, at least until next May."

"I won't," I lied. I had time to reflect on the short walk home. My date with the widow was three or four days away. I'd never talked about my personal life with her. How did she know about April?

My boss let me leave at three the day of the gala. "Even though you work in the back office, it will help you to see what the movers and shakers do," he said. "Stay sober and take good mental notes. You can debrief me later."

I was in the widow's neighborhood at five-thirty. The streets were crowded that hot September afternoon. A boy walking with his nanny dropped his ice cream cone. He stopped to cry. "At least you won't spoil your dinner," his caretaker admonished. I nearly stepped in the ice cream as I sidestepped the pair. I tucked into a bar to preserve my outfit.

Shiny shoes resting on a brass rail, I ordered a mixed drink, thinking I'd just sip it. "Going to the gala?" the bartender asked.

"How'd you know?" I replied.

"I've seen you walking dogs in the area. I figured the widow fixed you up with one of her friends' daughters."

"Hmph." I was afraid to lead him on, didn't want to be caught in a lie. My boss thought April was my date. April thought I was home studying. I like accounting because it demands scrupulousness. Now I was slipping into a morass of dishonesty. I drained my drink, raised my hand to ask for a glass of water. The bartender returned with another whiskey, "on the house."

I didn't have to finish the free drink, I try always to finish what I start. I glanced at the TVs, became engrossed in a soundless story, nursed my drink till I had just enough time to use the washroom and get to the widow's place at seven sharp.

I let myself in with the key I was to return that evening. Demon greeted me, went back to his corner to lay down. The front room was in disarray, filled with cardboard boxes. The Courbet sketch, covered in a clear plastic wrap, leaned against a wall under the window. I don't think I ever saw it hung in the widow's apartment.

"You're here!" the widow greeted me from another room. "Just give me a few minutes. I'm afraid we'll have to be fashionably late. Fix yourself a drink if you want."

I went to the kitchen, poured myself a glass of tap water then sat on the couch, examined the widow's famous study. The dogs in the picture didn't resemble Demon, a poodle mix, poodles were used as hunting dogs, not where I'm from, where Courbet's from, or so April told me.

"Excuse the mess," the widow said as she bustled about her inner rooms. I'm going to Buenos Aires at the end of the week. I can't take the cold. You'll be my last date in New York." As she said this, Demon approached me. I rubbed his sides, gazed into his big saucer-like eyes. I sipped my water, glanced at the painting then at Demon's importunate face. I envied his sobriety. "I'll be staying at the Plaza Tegui," the widow continued, "I've been there before, it's a lovely place. Perhaps I'll learn to tango, it takes two, I'll find someone if it's not too late."

Most women her age don't flirt the way the widow did. I imagined her flitting about her rooms, trying this on, taking that off, spraying herself, all to achieve that ineffable luminescence that so attracts businessmen and diplomats. I was charmed. "I'm not sure if I'll return to New York next year," she said. "I may summer in a sleepier place like Malmo. Don't be jealous, I can always send for you. You do get vacations. You're so young, so different from my other dates."

I imagined I heard with canine precision a clasp fastening.

Demon, still imploring, glanced at me, hung his head. "There, all set!" she exclaimed.

She was radiant as she entered the sitting room or so I surmise for I was already gone.

The Drunken Dragon

William Barker

my father drank his whiskey
with a small pour of ginger ale
in a glass depicting a red dragon
battling a bunch of Norsemen,
I would see the glass sitting in the cabinet
when I got home from school
and poured myself milk or water,
I hated that glass, hated what it represented,
sometimes considered hiding it,
or even smashing it to jagged shards,
but most times I'd simply stare
at this vessel seemingly docile in its lair,
awaiting a warm hand, cold cubes,
and the mead that turned my father
into a monstrous, drunken dragon
ready to burn down the entire kingdom.

Boom & Exhalation

William Barker

They're
all
dead:

Kerouac,
Bukowski,
Morrison,
Baudelaire,
Rimbaud,
Thompson,

some longer than others,
many before my birth,

I'm
unable
to picture them
in bones and bugs,
deep in the cocoa of Earth,
or ash, dispersed,

for on this rain-drenched night
in the belly of thunderstorms & woes,

they remain,
ALIVE,

familiar company to me
in the cheerful solitude,
music fleeing speakers,
fingers dancing
towards legend or obscurity,

and writing this I know,
I will soon be the same as them,
gone from this place
with a boom & exhalation,
leaving pages strewn
like the dismantled parts
of a time-machine
lacking instructions,

perhaps for grandchildren
to find decades later
inside sagging, dusty boxes
labeled with permanent marker:
Dad's Writing,

so many thousands of hours
under sun and moon

exhausted by their creator,

perhaps for new generations

of literary lovers,

caressing the braille

of immortality,

becoming lost

in the whirlwind

as I did,

once.

Scrub up

Colin Hankey

Bottle fed on Dettol

Swaddled in clingfilm to keep 'em fresh

Teflon Coated Kiddies

Never exposed to dirt and disease

See 'em run

And duck for cover

As I cough

And splutter

And sneeze

All get letters after their names

But nothing to do with a degree

OCD

IBS

And good old ADHD

Diagnosed and verified

by a quick search on Google

Reality TV Stars in waiting

They try to scrub their pains away

Control

Control

Control

The Order of the day

Refuse to grow up

Refuse to Grow old

Fantasy Football

Fantasy Wives

Fantasy Islands

Fantasy Lives

Scrub up

A Nip

And tuck

Before there's one grey hair

Now they are twinning my town

With Stepford

Clown Funerals

Dave Cullern

in a place
without landmarks
I can feel my skin
from across the room
as I hold court
with the imaginary interpretation
of strangers

my feet agitate
like the first flies of summer
and I feel familiar stories
against my palms
as I gesticulate
wildly

I wear the gaze of others
as unremarkable eyes
meet my own
and I feel the burning
of my family crest
through armour plated cotton

as this suit

tightens

around my neck

I relieve my hands from my pockets,

fold my arms across my chest like chains,

my teenage scars burst open

and wisdom teeth fill my cheeks

I state facts which I know to be true

in remembrance of that which I left at the door,

my tight shoes open beneath my clenched feet

and my toes tell tales of who I was before

Drew Campbell

"Inaccurate Meetings"

Timelines, blurring out.

Tangled through confusing space.

Vast glitches, abrupt.

"Read the Room"

The pressure confined,

Between layers of tension.

Eats the undertow.

Flowers

Nadja Moore

Arses and thighs

Keeping it tight

And loose

At the flower shop

Stand

Buying flowers

From the flower shop man

"I've been here since seven!"

Says the flower shop man

"It's been a long day,"

Says the lady buying

Flowers

Three women

In the space

Of an hour

Three

Young women

Bought flowers for themselves

"Men are dicks"

Say the ladies

Buying flowers

For themselves

One man

In tight chinos

(his bum at the bottom

Of the triangle)

Buys flowers

Too

What has he done?

Whose birthday is it?

Whose anniversary?

"Men are dicks"

Say the ladies

Buying flowers

For themselves

Flicking from one

Boy to the next

Looking for dad

Or the opposite of dad

Looking for love

Or the opposite of love;

You will find the one

Says the app.

He'll buy

You

Flowers

From

The flower

Shop

Man

On his way

Out

Of

The

Station

And

That

Still

Counts.

The lady behind the bar

Nadja Moore

The fire, the lady behind the bar
the bloke on table three,
fat and tired,
likes ham, egg and chips
on Monday night
before trying to convince
himself he may or may not
have a pudding. The pudding
in question isn't your regular choice
of pudding. It's a packet of mini-cheddars.
"Pudding," he'd say, nodding his head
at me before hoovering it up
in the space of a minute and
folding the packet into a spaceship
and throwing it into his empty beer glass.
I picked up the glass, nodded at him
and went to pour his normal
brew. The local favourite. Ranmore
ale. I brought it back to him and
walked off. His wife left him. He told
me all about it one slow afternoon while
I was scrubbing the bar. He must have

told a number of barmaids before me.

That's what a barmaid does.

She listens. Sometimes

the rich man shows you his watch

and says, "Guess how much it was".

Sometimes the middle-class man

grumbles, "Why do they_tsss_why did they do that?."

Sometimes the poor man says, "they told me

I had six months. I'm still here. Life, aye?"

And you just listen. You scrub and listen

and when they leave they look at you

with the tenderness of little pups, grateful

for your ears and breasts.

Death Faces of Death Faces
Kevin Tosca

A well-crafted piece of mail addressed to some former tenant arrived the other day. A catalogue. A *team*-building catalogue. Products for the team *builders*. Products with English names like Blast From The Past, Jailbreak, Lifeline, Leonardo's Ladder, and Strawberry Fields Forever. Products mostly costing in the two- to five-hundred euro range, but one product, The Juggernaut Express, priced at a cool 1,500.

Each product had its own page. Each page featured photographs of people playing with them, white people in their 20s, 30s, 40s, 50s, and 60s, i.e., working white people, working *white-collar* white people with smiles and concentration and *joy* plastered on their faces.

I couldn't look away.

This, I thought. Thiiiiiiiiiiiisssssssssss. THIS wasn't meant for me. I wasn't supposed to see THIS. No, not THIS shit. And THIS shit is THE shit. And this choice primo shit is MUCH more than paid actor pseudo-science. THIS shit is smoking gun. THIS shit is incontrovertible. This SHIT is a priceless document in the hopeless indictment of NOW.

Minutes passed. Hours.

Then I (literally) ran to my local McPaper, purchased a twenty-five euro paper shredder, dashed home and annihilated the catalogue before my wife and son returned because we are modern human beings and it is best to forget this.

2 pumps

Jason Gerrish

Loading our tools, from the company van
to our carts outside Mill Creek Pump House,
Big Dummy said, 'I fucked the hell
out of this chick, last night.'

'Whatever you got to tell yourself,' said DC.
'We fucked for 3 hours!' said Big Dummy.
And then Burke weighed in; said, 'My
wife calls me 2-Pumps, because when I'm
done drinking, that's all I got left in me.'

'How do you satisfy her?' said Big Dummy.

'I work all day, unlike you motherfuckers,
and *nothing* cuts into my drinking time.
I make up for it, on fuck night, every Saturday.'
'You got a fuck night?' said DC. 'Yup,' Burke said.

In any case, they let us in the pump house, to
the machinery that keeps the river from the city.
I said, 'God damn! Look at the size of them pumps.'

Burke said, 'That's right, boys, get a look, but don't get excited. You're gonna work today.'

Emetophilia

Jonathan S Baker

As a young girl
she was kind to fairies
and so pretty things
now fall from her mouth.
She punctuates her speech
by spitting pearls on the ground
or bursts into hacking fits
as the roses' thorny stems
are horked up
from the back of her throat.
Still though…
the prince is into it.

Parking Lot Interlude

Jonathan S Baker

Black currents of curls wash

over the shoulders of her uniform.

She is as sharp as the wind.

She is as brutal as the cold.

Fetid flecks of wet brown grime

dot the skin of his hands.

He is as empty as his wallet.

He is as spent as his change.

He grabs his prick.

She grabs her club.

He needs a place to sleep so he beats it.

She needs to keep the peace so she beats him.

She subdues him. She takes him in.

In the warm backseat of her cruiser, he smiles.

ALL OF THE GREAT POEMS

Martin Appleby

Sometimes I feel
like I have written
all of the great poems
I am ever going to write

Sometimes I feel
blocked, backed up and stuck
Totally bereft
F U C K E D

Then an idea'll hit me
out of nowhere
right between the eyes
or right between the legs

and I'll lay the words
down on to the page
and make those
motherfuckers sing

It is a sensation
that little else can beat
not quite as good as sex

but up there with a good wank

Sadly
this idea
this poem, today
is not one of those times.

The Gentle War

Chris Simpson

You start with buying a hi-vis vest. Dig out your worst clothes. Make sure your boots have seen better days. Don't shave. Get some quality bin bags, that's one area you don't want to skimp on. You also want a decent litter picker. Treasure it. Get up early. Awake at five, out the house by ten past; no shower. Take the bus to the end of the line. Once off, start your walk.

What could that crisp packet tell you about someone? Couldn't be arsed to put it in the bin, but hungry enough to eat every grain. Not a crumb left. Nothing. Telling stories, that's what people do even when they don't realize they're doing it. Pieces of paper. Adore pieces of paper. A drawing of something which looks like a robotic cow…you can get off on that for days. Getting closer to people without having to breathe in their lies. Receipts. See those all the time. Got two thick scrapbooks of receipts. Drink cans, you've flattened out a few - the ones which are exotic, which you don't usually find. The ones that are really unusual, where you can't make out the language, something Arabic you reckon, those you put in frames. Got a triptych of cans on the living room wall.

Then you get the stuff which is murky. Condoms. You don't know if they're full of some bloke, or full of some dog because you have an active imagination. You think of dogs who don't want puppies and the lengths their owners go to for their depressed pooches. Could get them snipped, but there's no imagination in that. Cut into the skin to kill chance, that's where that story ends. Bit of dreaming involved with a condom. Find used knickers too. Someone might jump to conclusions, that you use them. But that's not how this works. With used knickers you wash them, let them dry, inspect and maybe give them another rinse. When the washing is done, you iron them and keep them in a small drawer. Every last one of those knickers now smells of lemons. You correct the mistakes of others.

When did this all start? isn't an interesting question. More fascinating is to ask, *When is this all going to end?* You ponder. You don't press. This life is a gentle war. All you can say is, by the time you get home you've earned a cup of tea and a sandwich. You've earned a sit down. You've done something with your time.

People love to get rid of their lives. They do it every day.

Something About Everything is Killing Everyone
Steve Zmijewski

Pink sky calm.

Those stray birds that sing in the big neighborhood tree are

Hammering along.

I hear them,

Scraping fate from numbed branches.

It's a code red in my head,

Choking up over each, early star and shoveling slush.

Then arrives the snow plow, Without concern for the street

Or anyone lumbering around.

I can't relate to that notion

Or any view that could be found for simply

Pushing shit aside.

My chattering teeth overlap a

Frost petrified pout.

My mouth mumbles parts of words,

Your unfinished songs frozen in the air.

I had a daydream you died.

I was in the basement, my feet were still cold.

The phone didn't ring.

You were high in a tower and you died

Alone

Before I could get to you.

Before I could tell you, buddy, baby, I wish I was dead too.

Gumball Spider

Clay Hunt

I smoked a cigarette on my back patio.

I spit on a spider's web that infested the wooden railing.

My spit triggered a gumball sized spider

to crawl from beneath a crack in the windowsill.

I jumped back, almost dropping my cigarette.

I watched the spider check my spit for nutrients.

It crawled back into oblivion.

I admired the spider for knowing a giant roamed near its

home, yet still checked its web for food.

Imagine if spiders knew how much we feared them.

We'd be stuck to giant webs and slowly chewed alive,

as if the world weren't doing that to us already.

Valley Heat
Clay Hunt

I drove through the valley heat
around my old stomping grounds.
In corners of sketchy intersections,
teethless faces wrinkled by harsh realities
dug through trash cans outside of
Jack in the Box.
Drugs were bought and sold at
Denny's across the street.
My heart whispered through my lips
as the gas pressed down.
The idea of home proved glamourous.
The freedom of chaotic thought traded
dollar bills for snipes,
paychecks for trash findings and kind gestures.

My idea of home changed.
I used to snuggle in my sleeping bag outdoors
with a fifth of Black Velvet,
and Coast to Coast AM with George Noory,
on my FM/A.M radio hoping the batteries
lasted longer.

As I drove through Modesto,
I thought of San Francisco.
The ocean breeze felt so good every
day when it kissed my cheek
on the way home.

Now I lie in a bed made of bouquets.
Lavender blooms though our bedroom.
Migi and Kevin shed their hair on the hardwood floors.
The smell of kimchi fills the kitchen.

death avoiders

Jon Watson

death avoiders

and poets the

lonely poor ones

with gold word

emerald diamond amethyst

words to soothe

the word

addicts

imbibers of sacred old stanzas

lotus eaters pale opiated poetry

saints

death avoiders

soar druggd' above the corpse of

your

ordinary loved

chai tea and cigarettes

Jon Watson

books sit quietly

on their shelf

old grunge records

in their soul sleeves

I sit lonesome

Like Coleridge

or old Kerouac

a divine fragility

to read such beauty words

the drug was childhood

the comedown was memory

ANTI WAR RALLY 5/4/22
Danny D. Ford

the baby looked
at me

& I looked back
at the baby

it smiled
I frowned

neither one of us
had a clue what to do
about any of it

Waiter Poem #1
Danny D. Ford

a famous animal face
just above the clit

I take a pic
of my main
distraction

& show it to her
as we close up

later
her boyfriend
drives us home

"remember me"
Tohm Bakelas

he kept old newspapers
believing they spoke to him,
he cut out obituaries and
hung them from the curtains,
believing he knew the dead,
believing they forgot to say goodbye,
believing it all meant something

from floor to ceiling
he had rows upon
rows of paper
lining his apartment,

he had no radio,
no tv, no microwave
just stacks and stacks of paper

and everywhere he went
he picked through trash,
collecting shreds and
scraps and torn bits
of paper he believed
to be valuable

when they found him

buried beneath his life's work,

stuffed in his mouth was

a crumpled newspaper

with two words written

in black marker:

remember me

trading darkness
Tohm Bakelas

it is an outdoor bar in a
popular artsy shore town,
and i am here with friends
and i am talking to no one
and i am staring outward
at passing cars on the busy street.

two and a half hours before
i walked burning shore sands
in my black shoes and brown
pants and yellow flannel.

as it was before, as it is now,
i am sweating out malignant thoughts,
sweating out the years of internalization
and unbreakable madness that has followed
in good times and bad times and all times.

and i dream of walking away,
sitting in the sand and waiting,
waiting for the ocean to take me,
waiting and waiting and waiting.

but i am here in this outdoor bar,
with my friends, and i am talking to no one.

and the sun sinks down
below the horizon
and the streetlights
come to life.

The Penis Poet's Had Enough *for Jonathan S Baker*
Tim Heerdink

Sitting in a lounge chair
beside the speakers in Bokeh,
I find out the Penis Poet
has finally snapped.

They've had enough
of the bullshit.

All the voices
that used to be
in their head
have overflowed
to the back table.

With my eardrum blown,
Jonathan starts their set
with demonic screams
like a rocker in Hell.

That shut them up
for about the time
it takes for one shot

of whiskey
to be killed
before the next
marvelous stanza
could begin.

12 Grams

William Bolyard

I ran through the woods last night

Naked

With the foxes

Rain soaked my skin

I came across a house

All the lights on

Boxes half-packed

Food molded on the table

Pictures blurred

Rain picked up and I stood under the overhang

The house was halfway

Between the living

And the dead

Weird

Soon the foxes called me back

So I chased them back through the woods

Guess seeing all I needed to see

The streetlights came back on

And I was home

Cold

Wet

And wondering

Why?

Why there were no doorknobs on that house

John Dorsey

Easter Morning

jesus was dead

his beer belly out

his pants

his fat ass

not thinking about easter

or the overtime

a beautiful chickenshit

in spring.

Daddy

the wrong song

a whiskey chaser of belief

the first hard frost

of past & future.

Idaho is Starvation

the crumbs of promise

poverty builds mountains

coyote songs

no one stays

to pay the beast.

FOR BREAKFAST
Kevin Ridgeway

I smoke some coffee
& drink a cigarette
until I wake up,
the demons asking me
for a drag or a sip,
but they'll get
nothing & like it.

FREE FOOD

Kevin Ridgeway

my landlord
got us
fried chicken—
tons of it.
I eat it,
a dirty bachelor
with my bare hands
until I have to go out
and fend for myself
again, in search
of discount nutrition
in a human race
I am not going
to win unless
I slow down
and remember
to wash my hands
of all the grease
so my grip on life
does not get
too slippery.

A Child in Wartime
Paul Cordeiro

1.)

torrential rain

baptizes the daffodils

I'm rising

to more news of scorched earth--

voices stopped, lying on the street

2.)

Russian tanks rolling...

the sky lights up

on the darkest night

3.)

that a child fallen

face down in the street

and not a Dresden doll--

its porcelain head smashed

Jacob Louis Beaney

pea

The doctor informs me that I have an irregularly small
prostate. Normally men my age are as
large as a walnut whereas mine is about the size of a pea.
Perhaps I have finally milked it dry
after years of self-abuse.
Halfway down the street, it suddenly occurs to me that I had
forgot to ask: petit pois
or garden?

worm

When I tell people I once turned into a worm, they often ask,
was I on drugs at the time?
And I have to admit that I was.
But let's not let that detract from the meaningfulness of the
experience.
Besides, I had a witness.
Were they also on drugs?
And again, I must confess that they were.

Wind Chimes and Church Bells
Jason Ryberg

I'd swear I must have been
reeled in from the deep end of a dream
of what I thought was a Sunday morning,
sometime in early summer or late spring,

the sound of wind chimes and church bells
ringing from somewhere through the open
window next to my bed:

but it hadn't been my bed or my room
in over thirty years,

and it wasn't a spring or summer morning,
and there were no wind chimes or church bells,

just an alarm tone on my cellphone,
set to wake me to the slow dirge
of another January day.

Victor Clevenger

health clinic

he says an herbalist told him it could kill him so he considered
eating hemlock once...
jesus christ   this place is depressing

i keep telling myself

sitting through a crowded church service
still skeptical

thinking about

how nobody really knows
what they don't know

Some Chorus of Impermanence
A.S. Coomer

When I see mountains
I think of impermanence
How even crags crumble

What good are these words?
Inky black splotches
On the backs of cleaved trees
        Pulp, all of it

These snaggle toothed snarls
Of life & love & loss

Not to mention
        beauty

But then there's the glide of the pen
A nearly silent singing
Reverberating echoes of some chorus
Picked up & plucked
From a cobwebbed corner
Of the gray space
You try to ignore

& you find you already know the words

       Ineffable as smoke

       Liminal as running water

& you can't help but sing along

To hell with eternity

I, too, am a rock

A soft one, a minor one

But a part of the mountain

       After all

Leviathan

Chelsea Rector

The revolution is expensive to produce
All women go walking out into the ocean
The world slows a second

Waves will trip and play in reverse
The birth of subtler times give notice
In generosity, a hammock

Art is its own becoming
Where to much give is false security
In back problems there is terror

About chairs that move,
Three-hundred and sixty, plus degrees
A poem for my country

We are giving credit for trying
Whatever version of extinction is upon us
Weeping over unfinished masterworks

Tea cools down by tons, yet an undecided state
Cup a taxonomy of lines and shapes
And identify the following:

Classic forms of risk include
A frozen metal sharp-edged disc
Water tables carboning

Crazy storm
Every type of ship can sink
Even if the sky is blue

Contributors

In order of appearance

Available from Laughing Ronin Press

We Live The Songs – Steve Zmijewski

Waiting in Phnom Penh – Luke Young

Generation Zero – U.V. Ray

Upcoming from Laughing Ronin Press

Windswept – Paul Cordeiro

Cock of the Walk – Jonathan S Baker

Alec Baldwin Alec Baldwin Alec Baldwin – Victor Clevenger

www.ingramcontent.com/pod-product-compliance
Lightning Source LLC
Chambersburg PA
CBHW020603030426
42337CB00013B/1184